Lest We Forget

A Visual Memoir

Sandra Brick and Fred Amram

RAM INNOVATION PUBLISHING
2022 | MINNEAPOLIS, MINNESOTA

Lest We Forget © copyright 2022 by Sandra Amram Brick. All rights reserved. No part of this book may be reproduced in any form whatsoever, by photography or xerography or by any other means, by broadcast or transmission, by translation into any kind of language, nor by recording electronically or otherwise, without permission in writing from the author, except by a reviewer, who may quote brief passages in critical articles or reviews.

ISBN: 978-0-578-34112-5

Cover and book design by Mayfly Design

Library of Congress Catalog Number: 2021924718
First Printing: 2022
Printed in the United States of America

Dedication

We dedicate this book to Cousin Aaltje, murdered in Auschwitz, to the Musabende family, massacred in the Rwandan genocide, and to all the other victims of genocide who cannot tell their stories.

Fred's citizenship certificate, dated 1946

Contents

Fred Amram, Germany, circa 1937

Prologue

Holocaust historians ask us to remember the six million. Six million murdered Jews!

Six million is a number too large for most to understand. Try counting to six million. An unattainable challenge. "Six million" has little meaning.

Cousin Aaltje was one of the six million. She was gassed in Auschwitz at age 3½. That has meaning.

Paternal grandma Jettchen Amram was killed in the Riga Ghetto at age 70. Oma was one of the six million. That has meaning.

Uncle Herman and Aunt Karoline Müller, whole families, butchered in the Sobibar death camp. That has meaning.

A story well told has meaning. These 24 stories ask us to remember the Holocaust and all genocides, to remember our promise—our hope—of "never again."

Beyond the mass murder that is part of every genocide, refugee resettlement of survivors is another consequence. Hundreds of thousands of Jews left their European homes to escape the Nazis. Each refugee had to learn a new language and adapt to a new culture—to establish a new identity. No easy task. Each escapee tells a unique story of adapting.

Norbert Miller (second from right) with family, circa 1935

Three sisters with their aunt, Bertha Nussbaum. Sitta, the oldest girl, becomes Fred's mother. Karola (right), and the youngest, Käthe (front), circa 1918.

Else Nussbaum (Fred's maternal grandmother), circa 1956

Cousin Norbert Müller was 14 when he travelled to England with other children as part of the Kindertransport, leaving his younger sister, Susanna, and parents, Sebald and Laura, behind to be butchered in the Riga Ghetto.

Cousin Willi Müller was 16 when he escaped to Palestine leaving his parents, Max and Clara, behind to be murdered in the Belzyce Ghetto.

Maternal grandma Else Nussbaum escaped to the United States leaving a daughter, Karola, to be killed in the Riga Ghetto as well as another daughter, Käthe, and a granddaughter to be gassed and cremated at Auschwitz.

At age six, Fred Amram escaped with his parents to the United States to establish new roots, creating a new identity in a new country far from slaughtered uncles, aunts, cousins, and a beloved grandmother.

At Sandra's encouragement, Fred wrote short stories which she "translated" into visual artworks. Fred's vignettes, along with Sandra's art, became a travelling exhibition. Our next goal was to reach a wider audience with the message of NEVER AGAIN as we encourage people to become active upstanders rather than bystanders. This book became our way to broadcast that message.

Fred recounts some of his experiences in Nazi Germany and his efforts to become American. In this book and the parallel exhibition, Sandra Brick's art offers visual interpretations of Fred's early Holocaust experiences and then his experiences as a refugee in the United States. Joining verbal and visual art, Fred and Sandra provide a multimedia experience to help the reader become immersed in the stories, to share the events, to empathize, to feel, "I was there!"

We examine what it means to "become American." At first, it means becoming a "foreigner," an outsider—with all the disadvantages of not knowing the language, the culture, and the sounds made by those without a "foreign" accent. Becoming American means not being what one learned to be in one's former country—including the behaviors, the gestures that allow us to "pass" as one of the "insiders." For refugees, it also means coping with the pain one is escaping—to cope either by rejecting what happened or by integrating those experiences into one's new life.

Becoming an American means trying to fit in, to dress like one's neighbors, walk like one's neighbors, eat like one's neighbors. And so, to fit in, Freddy had to adapt to new foods, new hairstyles, new holidays, new values—new ways of behaving. Freddy had to become a different person.

Lest We Forget illustrates the pain and fear and joy and wonder—the emotions—of a refugee from the Holocaust adapting to life in America. One sees the bombs falling. One hears "the roaring planes, whistling bombs, and explosions. . ." Are these images exaggerated by a terrified six-year-old boy or have they been softened during the 80 intervening years between the event and the telling?

To a limited extent, the grammar of the telling becomes part of the intent of the story. The early experiences are told in the past tense. Fred hopes to close the door to his years in Nazi Germany. In the middle of a memory, just as Fred steps off the boat in America, the story changes to the present tense to represent a new phase in Fred's life. The final four mini stories are a retrospective written by an adult looking back on life. The tone and the grammar changes again.

The art Sandra created captures some interesting details. For example, when illustrating "Nur Für Juden," Sandra's lettering on her tiny bench replicates the actual font used by the Nazis.

Translation introduces challenges. In *Lest We Forget*, Sandra translates verbal stories into visual stories, verbal art into visual art. She creates a visual memoir about a boy's experiences during the early Holocaust and the aftershock of the youngster's survivor guilt and dislocation in a new land. Is her interpretation faithful to the stories? How can we judge? After all, each reader creates a personal translation. The reader internalizes each story and creates imaginary pictures. Each reader creates unique images—unique interpretations. Are the reader's images the same as those Sandra has created? Are the reader's images the same as those Fred intended?

Lest We Forget exhibit with plexi covers

These stories generate feelings inside the reader/viewer—at least, that's the intent. Emotions—pain, regret, pity, hope, fear, revulsion, joy—are part of the experience of reading this book and seeing these images. A story with a happy ending teaches a different lesson than one with a sad ending or one that leaves a bittersweet taste. The visual artist is challenged to capture the intended feeling of the literary story and, in the language of art, send the intent to the viewer. The story's feeling provides the message. What feeling does the story capture? What message does it send? Therein lies the translator's challenge.

In "The Reluctant Grownup," we read that the Gestapo took Papa's complete inventory of textiles, thus changing a room full of color into a stark white space. To create a visual translation of that event, Sandra collected a diversity of authentic fabrics from the 1930s, textiles with intricate and interesting designs.

Fred, however, does not remember designs. He remembers only solid colors. "I loved the colors from pastel pink to glowing red, from aqua to royal blue, from lemon yellow to grass green."

Surely Papa sold fabric with patterns and with solid colors. Both Sandra and Fred visualized the contents of the fabric room. However, Sandra decided to not use the authentic patterns from her collection. Instead, she dyed fabric in solid colors to reflect Fred's poetic memory. The translator made a choice.

The collaborative process changed over time. The project started when Sandra decided to create an exhibition of artworks based on Fred's stories about his youth. Sandra selected a theme or episode from a story she thought important or interesting, and created a visual translation. Subsequently, she challenged Fred to write a short version of each story or episode—roughly 275 words. The goal was to display a mini story with its visual translation so that the combination of creations resembled a book.

As the two discussed Fred's life during the Holocaust and as a refugee, Sandra raised questions that prompted new stories. Fred wrote. Sandra translated. As the collaboration evolved, Sandra found old photographs and snippets of conversation that called to her. She then took the lead and created a few visual artworks and assigned Fred a writing task. He became the translator.

"Empty Frames" is an example of a collaboration based on Sandra's lead. She showed Fred an empty frame and a stone Fred and Sandra brought home after travelling to Yad Vashem, Israel's memorial to the victims of the Holocaust. The image created a powerful statement noting that the six million dead cannot create a memoir, cannot tell their tale. "Now write a story," she challenged. Reluctantly, Fred created 271 words that became "Empty Frames," the final piece in this series.

The collection became an exhibition that travelled to museums, galleries, schools, and houses of worship, locally at first and then nationally. The travelling collection has grown from nine pieces and is now complete at 24 visual artworks with 24 mini-stories. Of course, one could tell more than 24 stories. Someday.

Sandra uses embroidered prose, prayers, and poems to embellish her work beyond the face of the art. As a gallery exhibition (www.LestWeForgetExhibit. org), the artworks are three-dimensional. Frames range from 2½ to 4½ inches deep, allowing the artist to use sides, top, and bottom to let her creativity flow around the artworks. Because prose on the sides of the frames is not visible in this book, we have added Appendix A to share the words not seen in the two-dimensional prints.

For the reader who closely reads the labels placed next to museum art, we recommend Appendix B. Here we list materials and techniques used in each of Sandra's pieces.

Finally, on a personal note, the collaborative process led to personal and intellectual growth. Our marriage bonds become stronger as we continue to learn from and about each other. We are, however, plagued with different work styles and dramatically distinct biological clocks. Fred hates deadlines and despises mornings. "Good morning" is an oxymoron. Sandra, on the other hand, is awake at the crack of dawn and works best when she's behind schedule. So long as we tolerate our workstyle differences, all is good. We accept each other as artists with differing skills. We critique one another with love and honesty and with the understanding that agreement is not a requirement—albeit a goal.

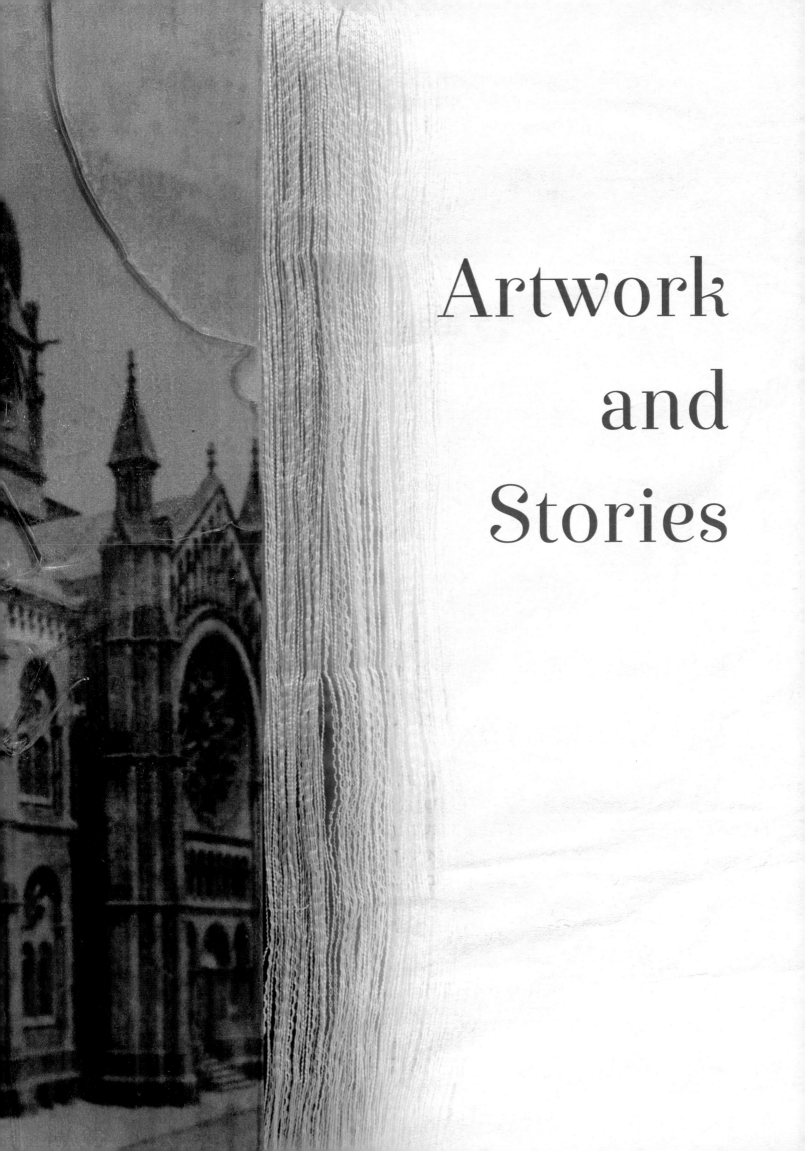

Artwork
and
Stories

Beglaubigte Abschrift aus dem Geburtsregister

Geburtsurkunde.

Aa.

Nr. 2006

Hannover , am 23. September 19 33

~~Vor~~ ~~dem~~ ~~unterzeichneten~~ ~~Standesbeamten~~ ~~erschien~~ ~~heute,~~ ~~der~~ ~~Persönlichkeit~~ ~~nach~~

XXXXX

Die Oberin des Mütter- und Säuglingsheims

~~wohnhaft~~ in Hannover

~~und~~ zeigte an, daß von der

Sitta Amram geborenen Nußbaum, Ehefrau des Kaufmanns

Meinhard Amram

wohnhaft bei ihrem Ehemann zu Hannover, Goethestrasse 25

zu Hannover, in genannten Anstalt

am neunzehnten September des Jahres

tausend neunhundert dreiunddreißig nach mittags

um achtdreiviertel Uhr ein Knabe

geboren worden sei und daß das Kind den Vornamen

Manfred

erhalten habe.

~~Vorgelesen,~~ ~~genehmigt~~ ~~und~~

Der Standesbeamte
In Vertretung
Wagner

Daß vorstehender Auszug mit dem Geburts-Hauptregister des Standesamts

zu Hannover I

gleichlautend ist, wird hiermit bestätigt.

Hannover I , am 22.September 19 38

Der Standesbeamte
In Vertretung

7a

3568

S

01. Righteous Christians

I was born in a Christian infants' shelter. My birth certificate has the signature of a nun. Her title is clear: *Oberin*. Mother Superior.

Just seven and one-half months after Hitler became chancellor of Germany, the Nazis had already prohibited Jews from using public hospitals. *Juden Verboten*. Jews Forbidden. Our Jewish hospital was also closed.

Some Christian agencies stood up to Hitler. My Mother Superior allowed Jewish women to use her facilities and encouraged her nurses to be daring. They took a risk on behalf of my mother and me.

Besides the nuns who assured my healthy birth, we knew other righteous Christians during the Holocaust.

When I was five, uniformed Gestapo regularly came to apartments of Jewish residents. They came to search for radios and other forbidden items. Most frightening was their search for Jewish men. Only the men in those early years. They took the men to. . . No one knew for sure.

When the Gestapo came to *our* apartment, Papa was always "out on business." Apparently, he had ways of knowing. He would disappear "downstairs." We lived on the third floor of a four-story apartment building. "Downstairs" he hid in the apartment of a Christian family. I carry the image of my tiny father fitting comfortably under a bed. I was never told the names of those risk-takers who sheltered Papa. Even in his later years, when questioned directly, he wouldn't reveal their names. They were simply "downstairs." Papa was still protecting these good people who had protected him.

In the home of these righteous Christians, these upstanders, Jews were not verboten. Jews were welcome. *Juden willkommen*!

02. Two Butchers

Kosher circumcisions require a professional circumciser, a *moyl*. Although our neighborhood butcher, Herr Mandelbaum, was not a certified rabbi, he had the special training of a moyl. He knew the ritual, the prayers, the cutting technique—and he had a sharp knife.

I was eight days old in late September of 1933. Family and friends gathered in our third-floor apartment to celebrate my *bris*, my ritual circumcision.

Butcher Mandelbaum said the blessing for washing the hands, for drinking wine, and for cutting. Jews have a blessing for everything.

After the prayers, he cut.

During the celebratory dinner, guests looked toward the windows when they heard music. A marching band. Uncle Max, the family tease, announced there was a parade in honor of my manhood. Imagine, celebrating a Jewish babe in Nazi Germany with a parade.

Our apartment had a small balcony and Mommy carried me outside to see my first parade. Crowds gathered on the sidewalks.

There were soldiers in gray uniforms and shining leather boots. There were drums and clarinets and all the wonderful brass instruments one expects in a marching band. Between platoons of soldiers, a long black open car appeared. A man standing in the car had dark hair and a mustache. Just as he drew even with our balcony, he saluted with an outstretched arm at a 45-degree angle. At that sign the spectators raised their arms and, with one voice, shouted, *"Heil Hitler."* The platoons of German military might echoed, "Heil Hitler." Mommy pulled us inside. Adolph Hitler was not a welcome guest at my bris. He was, however, the second butcher to attend.

Is there a blessing for two butchers at a bris?

03. The Chanukah Man

On the first evening of every Chanukah, every Chanukah before Kristallnacht, we lit the first candle. I used the *Chanukiah* that belonged to Papa when he was a little boy, a tiny menorah that required special tiny candles. With round Uncle Max on the couch blowing cigar-smoke circles, Papa announced that he needed to go to the post office for business. After a short while, the doorbell rang. Mommy announced with great surprise that the Chanukah Man had come. With a deep voice, he wished everyone a happy Chanukah. He was wearing a hooded green Mackinaw which he never opened. I sat on this stranger's lap, almost as frightened as when the Gestapo officers came to our house. Had I been a good boy during the past year?

I assured the Chanukah Man that I had been as good as I could be—allowing some room for error. Uncle Max, laughing aloud on the couch with his jelly-belly rocking, assured me that I was safe. Did I deserve coal for Chanukah? No, I was too well-behaved for that. In the end, the Chanukah Man produced a small toy—a lead ambulance that would ride on my uncle's belly when we played together or on my blanketed legs when I was sick. And then the stranger was gone.

When Papa arrived home, I complained that he was always at the post office when the Chanukah Man visited. I really wanted my father to meet this annual visitor.

When we arrived in the United States, we were too poor to have the Chanukah Man bring a gift. Instead, Papa gave me his small chanukiah to keep as my own. I used it to light tiny candles while he used a grown-up menorah.

Papa's menorah, now Freddy's

04. Nur Für Juden

Mommy and I window-shopped as we strolled to Hannover's Goethe Platz, an island of trees and flowers at the end of our busy street.

"Look. There's a hat we could buy for Papa."

"Would your father like that striped tie for his birthday?" But we never bought anything.

We saw a bright red dress that I promised to buy Mommy with my first earnings.

A few stores had the letter *J* painted on them. Others spelled out *JUDE*. I didn't understand why people were supposed to boycott those stores. Mommy always evaded my questions about the J. She just walked faster.

As soon as we stepped into Goethe Platz, I ran ahead to my favorite bench hidden in an alcove surrounded by tall trees. It was a shady spot and lots of birds lived in the trees. Mommy sometimes pointed to the nests, identifying types of birds. I gave them individual names like Gretchen or Hannelore. The birds whistled songs and Mommy whistled back at them. I think they liked Mommy's whistles.

Suddenly Mommy's eyes darted around nervously. "We have to go now."

"Why? We just arrived. I want to play with the birds."

"We must go now."

Mommy was looking past my head, so I turned around to see some letters printed on the top board of the bench. Letters that had not been there before.

I sounded out the short words printed on the bench. "*N-u-r f-ü-r J-u-d-e-n,*" I said slowly. Then I put the words together in a sentence. Only for Jews.

A week later all the other benches had words printed on them:
"*N-u-r f-ü-r A-r-i-e-r.*" Only for Aryans.

05. Reluctant Grown-Up

Three officers entered our apartment, all in calf-high shiny leather boots and all carrying drawn pistols. "Gestapo," announced the lead officer in his intimidating, black uniform. His visor cap displayed an eagle and a death mask–or was it a skull? On his left arm, he wore a red band emblazoned with a swastika. Pointing with his gun, he told my mother and me to stand in a corner. The other two officers holstered their guns and started searching my favorite room, the space where Papa stored the textiles he sold.

Perfectly white walls with perfectly white shelves showed off bolts of fabric in every imaginable color and texture. I loved the colors from pastel pink to glowing red, from aqua to royal blue, from lemon yellow to grass green. I loved Papa's fabric room better than going to the park, even better than eating ice cream. The colors made my heart beat faster.

When the officers had finished hauling away the last bolt of fabric, they looked at my mother, clicked their heels, gave a small bow and, in unison, shouted a *Heil Hitler*."

Mommy locked the front door, and we went into Papa's storage room. The glass chandelier made the white walls even whiter. All white! No color anywhere. We both cried. That was my last cry for many years.

The next time the men in uniform returned with their terrifying knock, I unlocked the door myself. This time I stood in front of my mother—not behind. I looked straight at the lead officer with my arms crossed. I guessed that was the proper posture for a grown-up.

Forced labor crew, Papa at upper right, 1939

11

For a brief moment I deserted you,
but with great compassion
I will gather you.

In overflowing anger for a moment
I hid my face from you,
but with everlasting love
I will have compassion on you.

Isaiah 54. 7-8

06. Kristallnacht

Any Jew living in Nazi Germany on November 9, 1938, remembers Kristallnacht, the night of shattered glass. From our balcony, I watched our local synagogue burning. I watched strangers kick Jews, easily identified because they were required to wear the Star of David. I watched police officers use their nightsticks to shatter windows of shops owned by Jews.

Papa disappeared as he always did in times of danger. I was told he was going "out on business," as he always did just before the Gestapo came knocking—and they knocked often.

How did Papa know?

Papa missed supper on Kristallnacht. I was allowed to stay up past my bedtime waiting for him to return. When Papa finally came home, he was carrying a huge bundle covered with large rags and a dirty brown blanket. Was it a body?

Papa removed the wrappings and I saw a Torah almost as big as my Papa. He had rescued the holy scroll from our local synagogue while the building was aflame.

My mother scolded, "Why take the risk? One should take precautions. And why bring a Torah into an apartment where even radios are forbidden? What if the swine come to inspect?" The swine, the Gestapo, were frequent visitors. "What will we do with a Torah in our apartment?"

Papa had no plan. "The rabbi will know what to do," he assured.

"Where does one find a rabbi on a night like this?" asked Mommy.

When I awoke the next morning, the Torah was gone. Papa was quite pleased with himself. I was only told that Papa had been "out on business."

07. Kindertransport

Not long after Kristallnacht, Britain agreed to admit almost 10,000 Jewish children from Germany and occupied lands. My granduncle Sebald and his wife, Laura, were invited to send one of their two children, Susanna or Norbert, to England. There the child would be cared for in an orphanage, a home, or other facility for children. No specific plans had been made for the youngsters. Laura and Sebald only knew that they had a chance to send one child.

Think like a parent. Do I send a child away to a strange country with a new language and to live with people I've never met? Will Great Britain be involved in the war? What will happen here in Germany? Where will my child be safest?

Having decided to send one child, do I send my son or daughter? Will my children ever meet again? Will I see my young traveler again?

Now think like a child. Imagine Norbert, age 14, the child chosen for the Kindertransport, as he sits on a train with other children on their way to a strange land. Each child has a small suitcase or rucksack. A few carry musical instruments. Will they ever see home again? Each child wears a nametag around the neck, an identification that tells the child's age and home address. A few children have special needs.

Before the war ended, Norbert, now called Norman, joined the British army and was among those soldiers who liberated Europe from the Nazis. He was not able to save his parents who were murdered with his sister on March 26, 1942, in the Riga Ghetto.

Norbert

08. Bombs Bursting in Air

Sirens signaled lights out. Every sturdy structure, including our four-story apartment

building at 25 *Goethe Strasse*, had a designated basement bomb shelter. Each night the shrill sirens woke us and, enveloped in darkness, we rushed to our refuge.

Our bomb shelter was cold, damp, and gloomy. Sometimes I gagged from the smell of urine and sweat.

One night when the sirens whined, my parents scooped up their "one and only" to join the others in the race to the basement. This time we saw a new sign on the door, "*Juden Verboten!*" Jews Forbidden! Now we were to experience the airplanes without the protection of the basement shelter and without the camaraderie of neighbors. Night after night we watched the sky show from our windows. Papa sometimes sat with me under a table.

The roaring planes, whistling bombs, and explosions in my head were far more frightening than the leaflets and the occasional real bombs. My small-boy imagination was far more dramatic than reality.

Papa believed that God would protect the Jews, believed it deep in his soul. Mommy had less faith. Her rage at "Juden Verboten" increased each day as neighbors, understanding the

message stopped talking to us—even avoided us. One night she cracked. As the planes came directly over our building she stepped onto our little balcony. She watched the bombs fall and the fires in the neighborhood. My mother looked up into the dark sky and cried out, "Dear God, please let the bombs destroy this building and these people. I will be content to die with them."

Quietly she added, "If they won't live with Jews, let them die with Jews."

09. A Freedom Cruise

In Antwerp, Mommy, Papa, and I crowded into a small cabin on the Pennland. Papa announced with a grin, "We're on our way to a land of milk and honey."

Our cabin had one little round window about the size of my face. Huge waves splashed against the glass. Rough seas meant that passengers on the tipping boat rarely visited the dining room. Nor did they visit the deck which was often covered with water. The fierce wind and rain followed us across the ocean.

I became the crew's mascot, a healthy little boy always hungry. When other passengers were sick, I ate in the galley with the sailors. Many of the crew spoke German and translated everything I needed to know. I learned English words like "chicken" and "fried potatoes" and "hamburger."

My new friends presented me with a toy U.S. army truck which I "drove" everywhere—the conquering military hero. I imagined victorious American soldiers riding under the khaki-colored canvas top that covered the back of my truck.

The halls of the ship were mostly empty because the sick passengers rarely left their rooms. That allowed great highways for my truck to travel. Together we turned corners, climbed stairs, and explored every cranny.

We passed the Statue of Liberty at 4 a.m. on the 15th of November, 1939. Papa took me on deck to see the statue, the symbol of liberty. With tears in his eyes, he whispered some words in Hebrew that I recognized from the Passover Seder, "... and God brought you out of the Land of Egypt, out of the house of bondage."

Deutsches Reich

10. Names

By 1938, all German Jews were required by law to adopt a middle name which was inserted on all legal papers and, especially, on the identification card one had to carry—always. That was the gray identification card with a large "J" printed on the cover. "J" for *Jude*! Jew! All Jewish women were required to insert "Sara" into their name. My mother became Sitta Sara Amram. Men added "Israel" and Papa became Meinhardt Israel Amram. Now I was officially Manfred Israel Amram. At first, I felt proud. But when the kids without that middle name wouldn't play with me, I stopped being proud.

As we step off the boat in New York harbor on that mid-November day in 1939, the immigration officials Americanize our names—officially.

"Name?" asks the man, gently.

"Manfred," I answer, standing as tall as a six-year-old can.

"Fred," says the official and spells "FRED" in his book and writes it on my entry permit.

"Name?" asks the official.

"Meinhardt," says Papa as he shows his papers.

"MILTON," the official writes, and Papa becomes American.

"Name?" asks the official.

"Sitta," Mommy answers, and she spells it, showing off her high school English skills.

"SARA says the tall, uniformed immigration officer.

Sitta rants and cries. She can only recall the "Sara" on her German identification card. Nazis use the name as a pejorative. All Jewish women have the same name—the same brand. My mother decides that she might just as well go to the concentration camp if she will be renamed "Sara." There is no consoling her.

The official means no harm. He looks at the small screaming woman and quietly spells "SITTA" in his book.

11. Three to a Bed

At the immigration center, we move from table to table. Mommy shows our papers and answers questions. The clerks wave us on. At the last desk, we show a certificate from our sponsor to a uniformed official.

"You're good to go."

"Go where?" asks Mommy.

The man points to a gate.

"But where will we go?" Mommy whines.

The man points again.

Mommy can read, "Exit." Her high school English carries us through many signs and questions from officials. Her question really asks where we will eat and sleep in the biggest city in the world.

"There," shouts Papa. He rushes to a man with a sign: "Amram *Familie*." The stranger speaks our language and tells Papa not to worry.

"I'm from the Hebrew Immigrant Aid Society, the HIAS," he says. "I've come to help you settle into New York City."

We walk a little way to a trolley that doesn't say, "*Juden Verboten*." The HIAS man pays the fare and sits. We sit. When he stands, we stand. We follow him down a busy street and into a small hotel lobby that smells like very stale food, mostly cabbage. We're shown a small, dark, dusty room with one bed and a dresser. The man explains that this will be our home until we can afford our own apartment.

The three of us will sleep in one double bed. Mommy decides that I must sleep in the middle, so I don't fall out. She insists I sleep with my head at the foot of the bed. I sleep looking at their feet which stick out from the covers so that I can breathe. Papa's feet smell like the egg salad he selects at the cafeteria. To be certain that my feet don't smell funny, I never select egg salad.

cues command The air-bridged harbor that twin cities frame. "Keep ancient lands, your storied pomp!" cries she With silent lips. "Give me yo

מה נשתנה הלילה הזה מכל הלילות

Warum unterscheidet sich diese
Nacht von allen anderen Nächten?

Why is this night different from all other nights?

We're in America now!

12. First Passover in America

It is April and our first Passover Seder in the United States. Here we are in a land of milk and honey. No more Gestapo. No more hiding. No more fear. We are living in a dark, poorly ventilated New York tenement. The living room window overlooks a tiny courtyard surrounded by bricks and more windows. The air shaft, perhaps 30 feet square, allows minimal light and limited fresh air. Sounds from the open windows echo in the four-story shaft.

The Seder table looks festive, the silverware gleaming. The open *Haggadah*, the re-telling of the story of the Exodus out of Egypt, shows a right-hand column on each page printed in Hebrew. The left column displays the translation in German.

We had escaped—father, mother, and son—via Holland and Belgium and two weeks at sea. Papa, a small wiry man with a huge baritone voice, sings the prayers in Hebrew as though he were on stage. Five feet one inch tall, thin and muscular from Nazi slave labor in road construction, Papa knows how to celebrate freedom.

We light the candles, bless the matzo and the wine. In my embarrassed, childish voice, chanting in Hebrew, I recite the four questions asked by the youngest participant at every Seder throughout the world, now and in times long gone. Papa sings about Moses and the prophets and about freedom then and now. This small man sings with a mighty voice.

"Shhh, shhh," hushes my mother. "Shhh, the windows are open. The neighbors will hear."

My father rises from his chair and stretches to his full height. "I'll sing as loud as I like," he declares in German. "Let them hear. WE'RE IN AMERICA NOW!"

Artwork from Papa's Haggadah

13. A Refugee Visits the World's Fair

Papa announces he will take me to the World's Fair. Mommy read about the New York World's Fair when we were still in Germany. She tells me that corporations have science displays. She talks about "chemistry" and "engineering," using words I've never heard before like "*Wissenschaft*" and "*Technik*." With her *Langenscheidt* German-English, English-German Dictionary she teaches new words in two languages and explains ideas quite new to me.

On the subway to the fair, Papa and I talk about what I might become when I grow up. "*Tikkun olam* is most important," says Papa. "That's Hebrew for 'repair the world.'"

At the fair, we visit many countries. We step into a building representing Japan. Japanese people are short like Papa and me. We sit on the floor and drink tea.

We see a radio with pictures called "television." We see a display showing how a future city will look. Papa keeps saying, "This is what a peaceful world can be like."

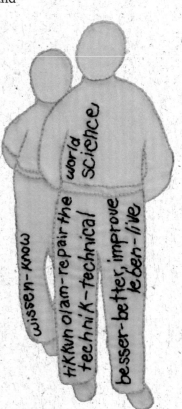

An industrial display has a huge mural two stories high. On one side of this enormous picture is a family scene from an earlier agricultural time. On the other side, we see a family living in a modern world of comfort. At the bottom of this mural is a banner with the words, "Better Things For Better Living Through Chemistry." I translate "Better Living" to "*Besser Leben*." From Mommy I learned that "chemistry" is a science. I say "Wissenschaft" and "Technik."

I promise Papa that I will study "Wissenschaft," whatever that means, so that I can help create "better living." Papa calls it "tikkun olam." Repair the world.

14. Bombs Bursting in Air Again

Wham! Bang! My head hits the school desk and then the chair to which the desk is attached. I'm the first to hide—the only kid in Mrs. Brower's 1942 second-grade class who knows how to respond to a New York City air raid drill. How am I to know it's just a drill? I'm a real air raid expert.

The other children look around to find the source of the shrill, whining cry. Mrs. Brower has been trained for this moment. Calmly she explains, "That sound is called an air raid siren. Whenever you hear this siren, I want you to quickly and *carefully* hide under your desks."

The "carefully" was surely added as a special caution after my painful and noisy escape into my cocoon. She explains air raids to the bewildered children. "You know that we're at war with the Japanese and the Germans. They probably won't come here. But, just in case. . ."

I don't need instruction. I remember hiding under a table with Papa when the RAF flew over Hannover. Airplanes loaded with real bombs that could blow us to smithereens. One of the girls starts to cry. From under my desk, I hear Mrs. Brower's words, warm, encouraging, protective. "I'll be right here with you." Her training manual has anticipated the children's fear.

Mrs. Brower's voice quivers just a bit. Perhaps she imagines the piercing whistle of a bomb dropping onto *her* school, *her* children. Even *her*self! Perhaps now, as she tenderly guides each of her charges under a desk, she imagines them as corpses.

I don't need to imagine an air raid. I have memories.

15. Today I am a Citizen

My name is called and I, a young almost-man, 11½ years old, open an elaborately carved door and enter a large, carpeted room. Behind the desk sits a gray-haired gentleman in suit and tie. A nameplate spells his name: "Mr. Jensen." The sign gives me a life goal. I want a job with a nameplate that spells "Mr. Amram." The man checks to see if I filled in the forms correctly. He addresses me as Mister Amram and treats me like the grown-up I pretend to be.

"Does the Constitution give women the right to vote?"

"No," I squeak in my most manly voice.

"How did women achieve the right to vote in the United States?"

"An amendment to the Constitution." I pray silently, *please don't ask which amendment*.

We discuss Abe Lincoln and the Civil War. Our interview ends with, "Good work young man. You passed. Congratulations."

I'm instructed to stand and to raise my right hand. I swear allegiance to my adopted country. Then Mr. Jensen wishes me luck and promises, "Your citizenship papers will be mailed in a few months."

On the next day, May 8, 1945, at a special assembly, the school principal makes a long patriotic speech. I'm afraid he's about to honor my new American citizenship. Instead, he announces that the war in Europe ended today. The Germans have surrendered.

On the way home from school, I pass a newsstand. I see a picture of a liberated concentration camp. Living skeletons. I imagine myself in the picture. I don't see a single child. Are all the Jewish children in Europe dead? I realize that, American citizen or not, I will always be a Jewish refugee. A survivor.

A·U·S·T·E·R·E

F·U·R·Y

SPECIAL IS WORTH DEFENDING

S·T·R·A·N·G·L·E

Mary Ann Grossman
763 Cherokee Ave.,
St. Paul, MN 55107

Two artists, Sandra Brick and Holocaust survivor, Fred Amram, explore a Jewish youngster's coming-of-age, first in Holocaust Germany, and then as a refugee in the United States. Brick translates Amram's bittersweet stories into poignant multimedia art works. Paging through this book walks the reader through an enlightening and moving collection of experiences.

—Anne Dugan, museum curator and scholar

The ink has hardly dried on the new *Lest We Forget: A Visual Memoir*, Ram Innovation Publishing, 2022. Amram's dramatic vignettes are sometimes horrific, sometimes amusing. In each vignette, reader and author share the experience. A tear here, a smile there, a little anger, a little warmth—the reader is absorbed into the stories. (An early version of one of the stories appeared in the AJW, many years ago).

With enormous insight and sensitivity, Brick, "translates" the stories into elegant art. Each full-page, museum-quality work highlights the nuances of the stories. One is led from prose to visual and back to prose, as empathy deepens. A powerful artistic experience changes the viewer into a participant who is reminded to NEVER forget and is empowered to accept responsibility to repair the world.

We hope you can join us on June 16 at the Textile Center, 6pm-8pm. Books will be available for autographing. The Textile Shop will be open at 6pm.

We plan an evening of stories, art, and great conversation. Here's a link to register for the rescheduled event. https://www.eventbrite.com/e/322211923537

We'd love to meet you at the book launch

Sandra

16. Spelling Lesson

A-U-S-T-E-R-E. Miss Christie explains during the first week of sixth grade, "Severely simple. Poor people have an austere diet." I conjure up memories of our last years in Germany. I understand "austere diet."

I stay behind when the Christian children go for religious instruction. Miss Christie, with that C-H-R-I-S-T in her name, leans close.

"How do you feel being left behind when all the other children leave?"

"I'm Jewish," I explain. She knows. Jewish is written on my forehead just as plain as the numbers on Auschwitz survivors' left arms.

"How do you *feel*?"

"Lonely. Different. Both."

"How does different *feel*?"

The war has just ended. I'm different from the Jews who were butchered and I'm different from my classmates.

"Let's not call it 'different.' Let's call it 'special,'" says Miss Christie as we end the school day.

After school, I'm invited to turn rope so that the girl I replace can jump.

A boy taunts me with "sissy." Albert embellishes with "sissy Jew boy." Others add "dirty Jew" or "dirty Hun." I'm both the German enemy and the "dirty Jew."

Albert punches me in the stomach. I drop the rope. He punches me in the chest. I haven't moved. "Sissy Jew boy," he repeats. He tackles me. I grab his arm and twist him around.

"You're breaking my arm," Albert whimpers. I don't hear him. In my head Miss Christie says, "Special is worth defending."

I place my right arm under Albert's chin and reach for my left shoulder. I squeeze. I recall, "How does it feel to be an outsider?"

"Anger," my brain says. "Rage." I squeeze Albert's throat harder. "Fury." I spell all the words as if in a spelling bee.

FURY. F-U-R-Y. FURY.

When I tell Miss Christie what happened, she reassures, "Special is worth defending."

17. Poconos Vacation

In the musty 19th-century hotel lobby, floor lamps stand at attention next to enormous, overstuffed chairs enveloping a few elderly men shielded by newspapers. The dark hardwood counter, elegant and worn, is staffed by a man in a blue uniform with lots of gold braid, designed for an admiral demoted to hotel clerk.

Papa, in his best broken English, announces with confidence, "We have a reservation for a week."

"Sir, we don't accept Jews or dogs," says the clerk.

Without missing a beat Papa looks to the right and to the left. "Jews," he shouts in a frightened tone. "Jews. Where are Jews?"

I recognize the trick. The clerk doesn't. Papa's act convinces the clerk that we're not Jewish. He apologetically explains that the resort has never allowed Jewish clientele. "Of course!" says Papa. "I understand."

I'm furious. I imagine the clerk speaking German. "*Juden sind hier unerwünscht.*" Jews are not welcome here.

The clerk begins to babble assurances about cleanliness and racial purity. He leans close to Papa, "The Jews control the banks and are greedy to the core." A momentary pause for air and the clerk wanders in a new direction. "Everyone knows that they rarely bathe. I can smell a Jew two blocks away."

Papa is ready to make his point. He grasps the clerk's forearm holding him close and in a loud whisper says, "My boy and I really are Jewish. It seems you can't smell us after all."

We leave after the manager returns our deposit plus a small sum as compensation for our trouble.

While traveling to the Poconos, I told Papa about the Lone Ranger and Tonto. Now, on the train back home, Papa explains that Tonto would not have been welcome at this hotel either.

18. Museum Trip

They don't allow Jews or dogs at the Pocono hotel. So, every day of our week-long vacation we have a different adventure. One day we walk to my favorite art museum.

This is my father's first-ever trip to a museum. He has a rural history. Papa certainly had little of the "culture" that comes with museums and concerts and big city life. Having left school after finishing fourth grade, he hadn't been provided with much opportunity for developing familiarity with the fine arts. Yet, for his young son, my father is willing to venture into a new world.

On the walk, I ask, "What is your favorite memory—ever?"

First, a long silence. Then, "The day our ship passed the Statue of Liberty. Our Freedom Day."

We enter the museum's Egypt wing and I explain the time frame and the culture of the pharaohs, a theme Papa translates to the evil pharaoh mentioned at our Passover Seder and the exodus out of Egypt—another escape to freedom.

We visit a room displaying early Italian Renaissance art. I love the massive paintings with rich colors. Papa relates well to the agricultural settings. He knows a great deal about horses and cattle from his childhood—new information to this big-city kid. We both marvel at the skill of the artists.

In a room dedicated to Flemish art, we come upon a Rubens painting. Three fleshy, buxom, naked women! I've visited them often with the curiosity of an adolescent. I've dreamed of touching these big-bosomed thrushes with their ample bottoms. However, on this visit I'm a bit embarrassed. What is Papa thinking? Papa, too, is in an awkward position. He is with his young son looking at a nude. I wait.

"Now there," my father announces, "is a woman who is built to put in a good day's work on the farm."

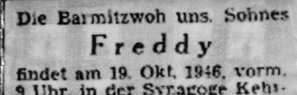

Die Barmitzwoh uns. Sohnes

Freddy

findet am 19. Okt. 1946, vorm.
9 Uhr, in der Synagoge Kehilath Jeshurun, 117-25 East
85th St. (zw. Lexington und
Park Ave.) statt.

Milton und Sitta Amram
geb. Nussbaum
315 E. 77th St., N. Y. C.
(fr. Hannover)

19. Today I Am a Man

I like Yorkville Junior High. After the last bell of the school day, I walk to Hebrew School. I'm in the last throes of preparing for my *bar mitzvah*—my passage to manhood. Rabbi Ruben coaches me to chant from the Torah and read my Haftorah portion. The words in the Torah are written without vowels. And I'm supposed to learn little squiggles, "chant marks." I continue to confuse these little scratches that tell me how to pitch my voice and how long I should hold the note.

On my big day, I wake up thinking, "Today I am a man." In my new suit, I walk to the synagogue. Papa and I take our seats in the sanctuary. Women must sit in the balcony so Mommy and my grandmother, climb the stairs. The main stage, the *tebáh*, is in the center of the synagogue, a raised platform. A reading stand faces Jerusalem. Long wooden pews surround the platform.

Several men take a Torah out of the ark that stands at the front of the sanctuary. They parade the Torah to the tebáh. The rabbi calls my Hebrew name.

I read from the Torah pretending I am a theater star.

Next, I read Haftorah. I hear myself reading faster and faster. I'm finished.

The rabbi recites the responsibilities of a Jewish male who has made the covenant. When I leave the tebáh I am a man. Papa shakes my hand. "*Mazel tov*," he whispers. I am taller than my father.

On Sunday I do my homework so that I'm ready for school. The reality of my "manhood" can be found in the old Jewish Haiku:

> Today I am a man.
> Tomorrow I will return
> to the seventh grade.

20. Denial

During the summer of 1960, my wife and I spend a few days in flourishing Munich. The war ended 15 years ago. We take a bus to the Nazi's first death camp just minutes outside of the big city.

Over the iron gate of the main entrance to the camp we read, "*Arbeit Macht Frei.*" Work will make you free. That's a joke. Perhaps death will make you free at Dachau.

We touch the barbed wire, no longer electrified. We visit the building where prisoners were stripped of their clothing, their possessions, and their identities. We see the building where prisoners' heads were shaved. Next door is a line of tall poles for the daily public hangings.

The crematorium building is unlighted and dirty, making it feel as sinister and ugly as the activity it housed. Several bricks around each of the ovens are loose and the iron doors are open. I look inside an oven to see where the bodies of men, women and little children were burned to ashes and black smoke. I look inside another oven and another. Am I searching for relatives?

Back at our tidy bed-and-breakfast, in German, my first language and my hostess's only language, I ask about Dachau.

"I've never been there."

"What did you think about it during the war?"

"We didn't know the camp existed."

"You're just a few miles away. Didn't you see the smoke from the enormous chimneys blocking the sun and the moon?

"Oh yes. The ashes fell on our windowsills. And the smoke smelled awful."

"What did you think about that?"

"We thought it was a factory."

The last stage, perhaps the crucial stage, of every genocide: Denial!

Exalted and hallowed be God great name in the world which God created, according to plan. Ma... and to all Israel. To which we say Amen.

21. Tante Beda Died Last Night

Tante Beda could love. Five feet tall and fleshy with a happy face. Her rosy cheeks needed no rouge. My aunt's big-bosomed hugs were always welcome. She was Papa's sister and had his cheerful disposition.

My mother mocked Tante Beda who hadn't read the latest novels—and never would. As a girl born in 1899 to a poor Jewish family in a rural German community, Beda received little schooling.

According to Mommy, Aunt Beda was ignorant, tasteless, boorish, overweight, and generally lacked "class." To Mommy, Beda's husband, Uncle Ernst, was a notch lower.

A few years after Uncle Ernst died, Tante Beda remarried. Her new husband, the widower, Chill Davis, was super-Orthodox, a trait my mother disliked. To Mommy, people were either not religious enough or too religious. While Mommy had not liked Ernst, she hated Chill.

One day in 1977, Mommy called my Minnesota home from Miami. "Tante Beda died in her sleep last night," she announced. "Chill is hysterical."

The funeral, two days out, was scheduled in New York City. "I'll see you at the funeral," I said.

Mommy's retort: "I won't be at the funeral. That Polack will behave without dignity. The service will be too religious.

"There is no reason for you to go either," she added. "You're busy at work. Your children need you. And Beda is not worth the expense of flying all that distance."

Uncle Chill and I recited the Kaddish prayer together. He was grateful that I attended Beda's funeral and for my spending a few nights with him. He kissed me. Chill never asked why my mother had not come.

Back home I thought about Chill's depth of faith and feeling. I thought about Beda's passion. The contrast to the façade that was my mother's life became clear. Had experiencing the Holocaust taught her nothing?

Juden ist das Geben
auf diesem Fußsteig
verboten
Żydom nie wolno chodzić
po tym chodniku.

Umgang mit Juden
Ausschluss aus der
Dorfgemeinschaft.

CHRISTIA
ONLY
JEWS NOT
ALLOWED
DANGER

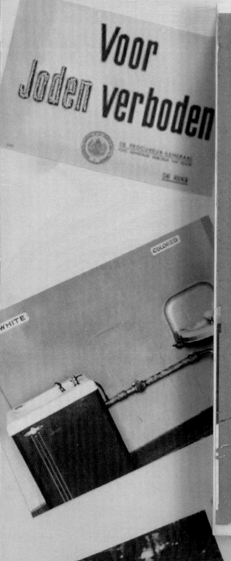

Voor
Joden verboden

COLORED

WHITE

V
FÜR JUDEN VE

COLORED
WAITING ROOM

Nur für Juden!

Juden
sind hier
unerwünscht

Nicht für Juden

22. Baker Freddy

Relating to Papa was easy. He treated me like a kid brother when he lent me his ties and when he insisted on buying expensive clothes for me. As I grew older, he liked to discuss world affairs and to ask my advice. I'm sure that if he were broke, he would be comfortable borrowing money from me. Of course, he'd use the cash to buy me new shirts or a suit with two pairs of pants.

Mommy was different. To her I was always a baby. My mother expected that I address her as Mommy even when she was 90 years old. I was always her "Freddy." She couldn't complain enough about my scuffed shoes. "Do you have a clean handkerchief?" sounds as strange to a 60-year-old son as "Stand up straight." "You should eat more" and "You're gaining too much weight" were part of the same conversation.

My parents brought almost nothing from Germany. Everything was lost. We each arrived with a small suitcase. My mother's contained a few photos, mostly baby pictures. Not a month went by that she didn't bring out pictures of me in a baker's hat. In my mother's mind, I stopped growing the moment those pictures were snapped.

I was a cute youngster when my mother's world turned sour. It was then that "*Juden Verboten,*" Jews Forbidden, first appeared on the trolley that passed our house. It was then that all but one of the benches in our local park were segregated with signs like "*Nur für Arier.*" Only for Aryans.

I was a cute little boy in a child's-play baker's hat when Mommy's world was arrested by the Nazis.

23. Cousin Aaltje

I'm an only child. It was customary for young German-Jewish adults during the Holocaust to have only one child—often none at all. "Why bring more Jewish children into a world like this?" my mother often asked. "Why, indeed."

My mother's youngest sister, Käthe—Mommy called her the baby—moved to Amsterdam and married a Dutch man, Isaak Wurms. Their only child, my only first cousin, Aaltje, was born in Holland on August 21, 1939, when Holland still seemed like a safe country for Jews.

What can I tell about Aaltje Wurms? All I remember is that she was small, an infant, when I saw her last. I can only imagine her life story, what might have been.

Might she have become a President, a Prime Minister, a Supreme Court judge? A Nobel laureate scientist? Or, might she have become a housewife caring for her own children and grandchildren? She might have grown old, just as I have. She might have grown old with me—just six years my junior.

The Nazis invaded Holland on May 10, 1940. We don't know the details of the family's suffering. Years later, however, while studying records at Yad Vashem in Jerusalem, I learned that on February 19, 1943, Aaltje, with her 29-year-old mother, died in an Auschwitz gas chamber. The Nazi killers had kept scrupulous documentation in a clear script. Aaltje's age at the time of her murder: 3½.

Parents gone. Uncles and aunts gone. Cousin Aaltje gone. I am an only child. All I have left is the photograph of a child who did not survive the Holocaust.

24. Empty Frames

I want to tell a story about my Oma Jettchen, my grandma, Papa's mother. I was a young boy when I saw her last. I sat on her lap when she read *Rotkappchen* and *Rumpelstilzchen* and let me turn the pages of her books. She was murdered by the Nazis in the Riga Ghetto. I grew up without my Oma.

As a survivor, I can tell my life story. I can write a memoir. Oma Jettchen didn't survive. I have no Oma story. I can't paint an Oma portrait. Just an empty frame.

My friend Alice Musabende witnessed the genocide in Rwanda. One day she arrived home from an errand to find the dead bodies of her grandparents, her mother and father, her twelve-year-old sister and her nine-year-old and two-year-old brothers. Alice was fourteen.

Alice survived and grew to be a successful adult. Like me, she writes about her life and her assimilation into a new culture. But her siblings have no story to tell. Her parents can't boast about their children or Alice's wedding or the day her first baby was born. Just empty frames.

How many families—mother, father, children—walked into the Auschwitz gas chambers? Only the smoke from the crematoria chimneys can tell how many whole families died with not a single survivor. Dead children have no story to tell. Dead parents and grandparents and uncles and aunts. Millions of frames forever empty.

Jews leave a stone when visiting a grave. I don't know where to leave my stone for Uncle Jacob or Aunt Karola or Cousin Aaltje. Can I leave a stone in an empty frame?

Appendices

Freddy with family in Germany, circa 1935

Appendix A
Additional Prose

Sandra uses embroidered prose, prayers, and poems to embellish her work beyond the face of the art. As a gallery exhibition, the artworks are three-dimensional. Frames range from 2½ to 4½ inches deep, allowing the artist to use sides, top, and bottom to let her creativity flow around the artworks. Because prose on the sides of the frames is not visible in this book, we share some of the words here.

02. Two Butchers

"Just as he has entered into the covenant, so too may he enter into Torah, into marriage and into good deeds."
>—Prayer said at Freddy's circumcision, September 27, 1933, Hannover, Germany.

11. Three to a Bed

"The New Colossus"
>—a sonnet by American poet Emma Lazarus (1849–1887)

Not like the brazen giant of Greek fame,
With conquering limbs astride from land to land;
Here at our sea-washed, sunset gates shall stand
A mighty woman with a torch, whose flame
Is the imprisoned lightning, and her name
Mother of Exiles. From her beacon-hand
Glows world-wide welcome; her mild eyes command
The air-bridged harbor that twin cities frame.

"Keep, ancient lands, your storied pomp!" cries she
With silent lips. "Give me your tired, your poor,
Your huddled masses yearning to breathe free,
The wretched refuse of your teeming shore.
Send these, the homeless, tempest-tost to me,
I lift my lamp beside the golden door!"

15. Today I Am a Citizen
Pledge of Allegiance (pre-1954)

I pledge allegiance to the flag of the United States of America, and to the Republic for which it stands, one nation indivisible, With liberty and justice for all.

19. Today I Am a Man

Today I am a man. Tomorrow I will return to the seventh grade.
　　—Bar Mitzvah Haiku.

Die Barmitzwoh uns. Sohnes

Freddy

findet am 19. Okt. 1946, vorm. 9 Uhr, in der Synagoge Kehilath Jeshurun, 117–25 East 85th St. (zw. Lexington und Park Ave.) statt.

Milton und Sitta Amram geb. Nussbaum
315 E. 77th St., N. Y. C.
(fr. Hannover)

Newspaper announcement from the *Aufbau*

21. Tante Beda Died Last Night
Mourner's Kaddish

Exalted and hallowed be God's great name in the world which
God created, according to plan.
May God's majesty be revealed in the days of our lifetime
Blessed, praised, honored, exalted, extolled, glorified, adored, and lauded
be the name of the Holy Blessed One, beyond all earthly words and songs of
blessing, praise, and comfort. To which we say Amen.
May there be abundant peace from heaven, and life, for us and all Israel, to
which we say Amen.
May the One who creates harmony on high, bring peace to us and to all Israel.
To which we say Amen.

יִתְגַּדַּל וְיִתְקַדַּשׁ שְׁמֵהּ רַבָּא. בְּעָלְמָא דִּי בְרָא כִרְעוּתֵהּ, וְיַמְלִיךְ מַלְכוּתֵהּ בְּחַיֵּיכוֹן
וּבְיוֹמֵיכוֹן וּבְחַיֵּי דְכָל בֵּית יִשְׂרָאֵל, בַּעֲגָלָא וּבִזְמַן קָרִיב, וְאִמְרוּ אָמֵן.

יְהֵא שְׁמֵהּ רַבָּא מְבָרַךְ לְעָלַם וּלְעָלְמֵי עָלְמַיָּא.

יִתְבָּרַךְ וְיִשְׁתַּבַּח וְיִתְפָּאַר וְיִתְרוֹמַם וְיִתְנַשֵּׂא וְיִתְהַדָּר וְיִתְעַלֶּה וְיִתְהַלָּל שְׁמֵהּ
דְּקֻדְשָׁא בְּרִיךְ הוּא, לְעֵלָּא מִן כָּל בִּרְכָתָא וְשִׁירָתָא תֻּשְׁבְּחָתָא וְנֶחֱמָתָא, דַּאֲמִירָן
בְּעָלְמָא, וְאִמְרוּ אָמֵן.

יְהֵא שְׁלָמָא רַבָּא מִן שְׁמַיָּא, וְחַיִּים עָלֵינוּ וְעַל כָּל יִשְׂרָאֵל, וְאִמְרוּ אָמֵן.

עֹשֶׂה שָׁלוֹם בִּמְרוֹמָיו, הוּא יַעֲשֶׂה שָׁלוֹם עָלֵינוּ וְעַל כָּל יִשְׂרָאֵל, וְאִמְרוּ אָמֵן.

23. Cousin Aaltje

"Thou shalt not be a victim. Thou shalt not be a perpetrator. Above all, thou
shalt not be a bystander."
　　—Yehuda Bauer

Appendix B
Material & Techniques

01. Righteous Christians

Images printed on cotton fabric; hand embroidered star with hand-dyed floss

02. Two Butchers

Photo collage image printed on cotton fabric; hand-dyed floss stitched around Sitta Amram, Fred's mother

03. The Chanukah Man

Hand-dyed aida cloth (an open, even-weave fabric traditionally used for cross-stitch embroidery); hand-dyed embroidery floss; Milton Amram's (Fred's father) menorah

04. Nur Für Juden

Hand-dyed silk ribbon leaves; two layers of hand-made paper; polymer clay bird and bench; vinyl lettering; blue paint; hand-made paper tree reinforced with copper wire

05. Reluctant Grown-up

Hand-dyed assorted fabrics; image printed on fabric; hand embroidered outline of Sitta and Freddy

06. Kristallnacht

Hand-dyed aida cloth (an open, even-weave fabric traditionally used for cross-stitch embroidery) and embroidery floss; image printed on cotton fabric; broken glass

07. Kindertransport

Hand-dyed floss; images printed on cotton fabric; trapunto (a method of quilting that is also called "stuffed technique." A puffy, decorative feature, trapunto utilizes at least two layers, the underside of which is slit and padded, producing a raised surface) embroidery of Fred's cousin Norbert

08. Bombs Bursting in Air

Stitch shibori (a Japanese manual resist-dyeing technique); doll house fencing; yellow paint

09. A Freedom Cruise

Image printed on cotton fabric; hand-dyed floss; toy army truck

10. Names

Photo collage image printed on cotton fabric; hand-dyed floss

11. Three to a Bed

Image printed on cotton fabric; embroidery; three in the bed image by graphic artist, Blue Delliquanti; embroidery aida cloth ribbon (an open, even-weave fabric traditionally used for cross-stitch embroidery); yellow paint

12. My First Passover in America

Hand-dyed aida cloth (an open, even-weave fabric traditionally used for cross-stitch embroidery); graduation hand-dyed floss; Haggadah from Germany

13. A Refugee Visits the World's Fair

Images printed on cotton fabric; hand-dyed floss

14. Bombs Bursting in Air Again

Hand-made paper; figures made from hand-made paper; doll house school desk

15. Today I Am a Citizen

Images printed on cotton fabric; embroidery with nylon thread; hand-beaded star

16. Spelling Lesson

Images printed on cotton fabric; hand-dyed floss; embroidery; aida cloth (an open, even-weave fabric traditionally used for cross-stitch embroidery)

17. Pocono Vacation

Photo collage image printed on cotton fabric; hand-dyed floss

18. Museum Trip

Images printed on cotton fabric; hand-dyed floss; embroidery

19. Today I Am a Man

Images printed on cotton fabric; hand-beading with glass beads

20. Denial

Photo manipulated with PhotoShop; all images printed on cotton fabric

21. Tante Beda Died Last Night

Embroidery; ribbon of aida cloth (an open, even-weave fabric traditionally used for cross-stich); hand-dyed embroidery floss; wool felt

22. Baker Freddy

Photo manipulated with PhotoShop; all images printed on cotton fabric; hand-dyed embroidery floss; Freddy is outlined with nylon thread

23. Cousin Aaltje

Images printed on cotton fabric, hand-dyed yellow cotton fabric

24. Empty Frame

Hand distressed frame using coffee, nail, and chain; stone from Yad Vashem (Israel's official memorial to the victims of the Holocaust)

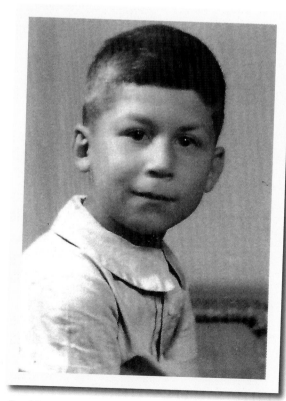

Fred Amram, Germany, circa 1937

Acknowledgments

We thank Katie Brick for acting as a bridge to the Greater Milwaukee Foundation which allowed us to transform a collection of art into a travelling exhibition. As Donald Brick contributed his tools, space and woodworking skills, Sandra apprenticed alongside him and, in the process, bonded with her father, learning yet more family stories. Feedback from fellow artists guided our decision-making. Fred's writing group provided ideas and support. Many friends acted as visual editors. We are enormously grateful to Ellen Weingart who read and re-read Fred's prose, shaping our thoughts, teasing out meanings and artful phrases.

We also remember Pat Brick who died while this book was developing. Pat, Sandra's first art teacher was a constant inspiration and a model for creativity.

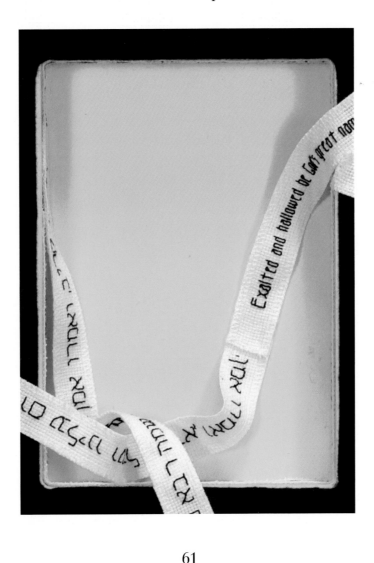

61

About the Artists

Sandra Brick is a fiber artist. Her work is part of the Minneapolis Institute of Art collection and can be seen at fine art galleries and shops. She has taught workshops and exhibited on three continents.

Sandra's fascination with "what if?" led to a degree in design from the University of Minnesota, an interest in applying her curiosity to visual art, and in sparking her sense of wonder in others. Currently, Sandra teaches classes and workshops at the Textile Center and responds to commission requests

Fred Amram is a retired award-winning professor, an inventor, a sought-after public speaker, and a much-lauded storyteller. In presenting Fred the Patent and Trademark Office's prestigious Excellence in Education Award, the Commissioner referred to him as "excellence in education personified."

Fred has authored five books, multiple book chapters as well as dozens of essays, articles, and stories published in diverse scholarly and literary journals. Holy Cow! Press published his recent memoir *We're In America Now: A Survivor's Stories*.

Visit www.LestWeForgetExhibit.org and learn more about the exhibit.